The WANTED

Me & You

INTRODUCING The W

Tom, Max, Siva, Jay and Nathan . . .

. . . five very different guys put together to form one incredible pop sensation. They make up The Wanted, the biggest success story of the year. The Wanted were formed by the management of The Saturdays, who scouted far and wide and auditioned hundreds of hot, talented guys in their search for the perfect combination, and I think we all agree that they certainly found it!

When the final five were chosen, they moved into a ramshackle pad in south London. And it didn't take long before they became more than boys in a band – they became proper mates, cooking for each other, eating, sleeping, singing and dancing together! But how did they pass their auditions and how did they manage to hit the top with their very first single? And, more importantly, who has a girlfriend and whose is the messiest room? Read on to find out answers to all these questions - and more!

MEET THE BOYS

Siva

Nathan

Tom

Max

Jay

@PARTY ANIMAL TOM!

#Name Tom Parker
#Date Of Birth 4 August 1988
#Height 5'10"
#Eye Colour Hazel
#Hair Colour Brown
#Hometown Bolton
#Star Sign Leo
#Favourite Food Indian, Italian
#Favourite Bands Oasis, Stereophonics
#Football Team Bolton Wanderers
#Favourite Animal Parrot
#Favourite TV Show as a Kid *Rosie and Jim*
#Favourite TV Show Now *The Inbetweeners*
#Dream Woman Mollie King from The Saturdays
#Twitter http://twitter.com/tomthewanted

★ ★ ★

TOM HAS A THIN FRINGE SO IN A PHOTOSHOOT HE HAD TO WEAR HAIR EXTENSIONS, MUCH TO THE AMUSEMENT OF THE OTHER MEMBERS. AWWW!

★ ★ ★

DESPITE RUMOURS IN THE PRESS, TOM IS NOT A SMOKER!

@HOT STUFF SIVA!

#Name Siva Kaneswaran
#Date Of Birth 16 November 1988
#Hometown Ireland
#Star Sign Scorpio
#Favourite Food Shepherd's pie, brownies, stew
#Height 6'1"
#Eye Colour Brown (tall, dark and handsome)
#Hair Colour Black with a few ginger hairs
#Favourite Band Switchfoot
#Football Team Manchester City or Bolton
#Favourite Animal Dog
#Favourite TV Show as a Kid *Buffy the Vampire Slayer*
#Favourite TV Show Now *Family Guy*
#Dream Woman Beyoncé
#Twitter http://twitter.com/sivathewanted

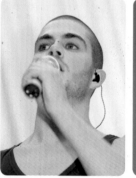

@FOOTY MAD MAX!

#Name Maximillian Alberto George
#Date Of Birth 6 September 1988
#Hometown Manchester
#Star Sign Virgo
#Favourite Food Dominos, full English breakfast,
  rare steak
#Height 5'8"
#Eye Colour Grey/blue
#Hair Colour Dark brown
#Favourite Band Queen
#Football Team Manchester City
#Favourite Animal Great white shark
#Favourite TV Show as a Kid *The Turtles*
#Favourite TV Show Now *The X Factor*
#Dream Woman Sinitta
#Twitter http://twitter.com/maxthewanted

@BAND BABY NATHAN!

#Name Nathan James Sykes
#Date Of Birth 18 April 1993
#Hometown Gloucester
#Star Sign Aries
#Favourite Food Spag bol, Chinese, soup, roast dinners
#Height 5' 9"ish
#Eye Colour Green/blue
#Hair Colour Brown
#Favourite Band Boyz II Men
#Football Team Manchester United
#Favourite Animal Cat
#Favourite TV Show as a Kid *Match of the Day!*
#Favourite TV Show Now *Britain's Got Talent*
#Dream Woman Kate Thornton
#Twitter http://twitter.com/NathanTheWanted

@DANCING FEET JAY!

#Name James McGuiness
#Date Of Birth 24 July 1990
#Hometown Nottingham
#Star Sign Leo
#Favourite Food Pizza, pasta and pesto, chips, cheese
  toasties (Jay is vegetarian)
#Height 6'1"
#Eye Colour Blue
#Hair Colour Brown
#Favourite Band Coldplay, Newton Faulkner, Florence,
  Jack Penate, Damien Rice, Justin Timberlake
#Favourite TV Show as a Kid *How 2*, Carol Vorderman
  is there anything you didn't teach us?!
#Favourite TV Show Now *Misfits*
#Dream Woman Vanessa from The Saturdays
#Twitter http://twitter.com/jaythewanted

THE ROAD TO SUCCESS

A few years ago, the pop music scene was changed when a group of cheeky chaps from London – JLS – made it to the second round in *The X Factor* and went on to smash their way to the top of the charts and sell out arenas across the UK. Suddenly, boybands were cool again! But apart from JLS, there was no one else on the scene.

The scouts are out!

So the masterminds behind girlband The Saturdays were dreaming up another scheme – to put together a boyband to rival the girls' success! They advertised in a magazine and received scores of applicants – all hot boy talent hungry for a slice of pop music pie!

Although The Wanted smashed the top of the charts with their first single, no-one was more surprised about that than the boys themselves. Mere months earlier, the boys had been living ordinary lives, just dreaming of success.

'WE'VE GOT NO TIME FOR CHEESE. WE'RE JUST FIVE LADS HAVING FUN! YOU WON'T FIND US SITTING ON STOOLS IN OUR SUITS AND STANDING UP FOR THE KEY CHANGE!' NATHAN

Life before fame

TOM

Tom auditioned for *The X Factor* in 2007 and was booted off in the first round by a producer – he didn't even make it through to see Simon Cowell and the other judges. Can you believe it? After that he'd worked in McDonalds, but the audition for The Wanted had been the first he'd done since *The X Factor*.

MAX

Max was the only member who'd had some experience of the industry before, when his band Avenue were kicked off *The X Factor* in 2006 for having a manager. Max was devastated, but consoled himself with his back-up career of football. Then bad went to worse when a hip injury meant Max had to give that up too.

JAY

After finishing college, twinkle-toed Jay attended audition after audition, trying to get a break in the industry. His dance training had paid off – he was magic on the dancefloor, but getting work was proving difficult. In the meantime, Jay worked as a waiter and he also sold keyrings in a nightclub to make a little cash to get by.

NATHAN

When Nathan saw the advert, he was only 16 and still at school. But he'd always been a talented musician, having played the piano, written songs and played the bagpipes from a young age! Nathan was asked to audition for the group after he'd impressed teachers at the Sylvia Young Theatre School.

SIVA

Half-Sri Lankan and half-Irish Siva spent his days modeling with his twin brother Kumar, as well as working in a local museum and writing songs on his guitar. Siva was spotted on the agency's books and caught the eye of The Saturday's management, who asked him to come along and audition.

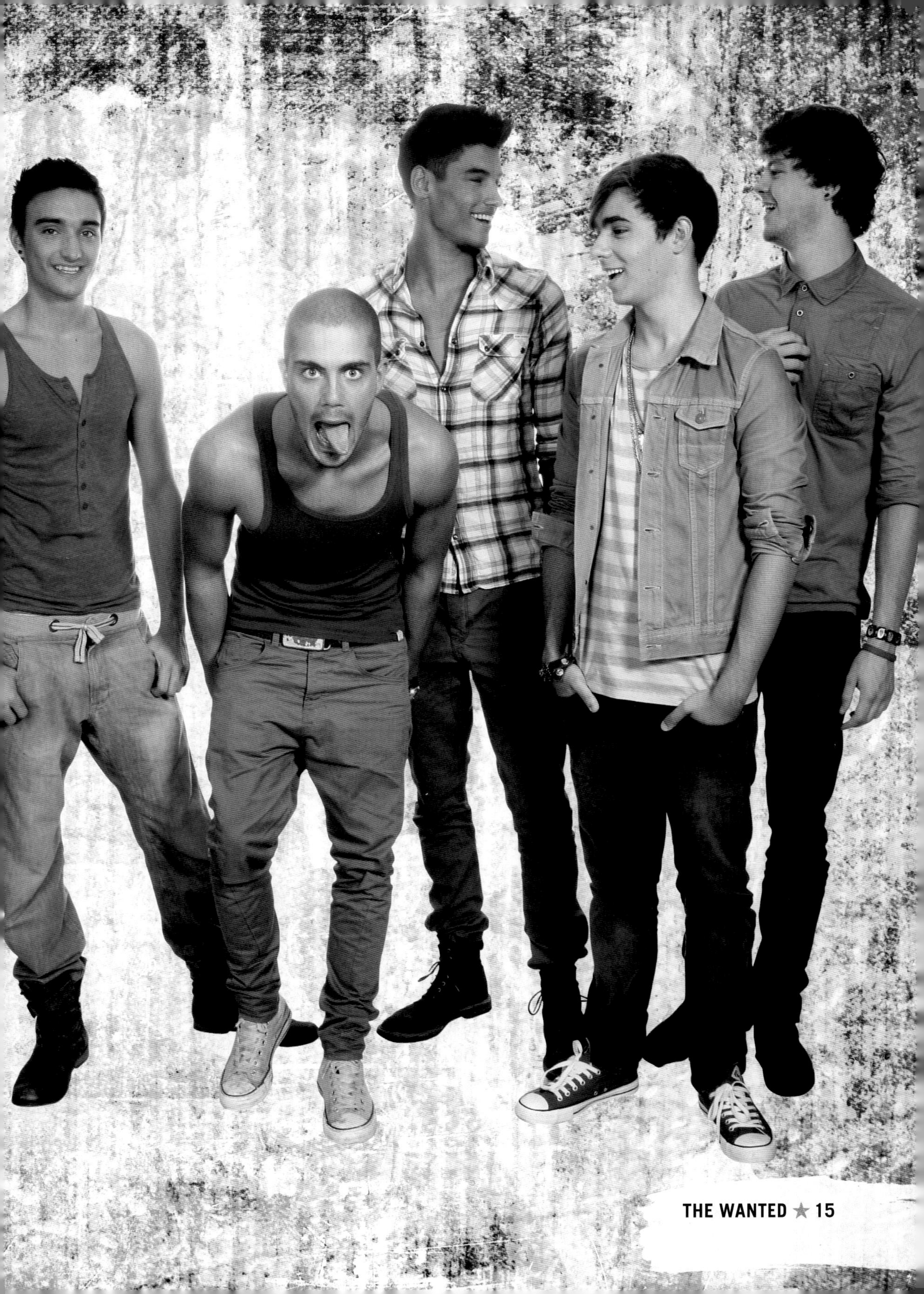

Finding their feet

Tom, Jay and Nathan attended the auditions from the very beginning, later joined by Max and finally Siva. When the boys first met each other, they were pretty nervous, as you can imagine. 'As soon as Siva came in, I wanted to leave,' joked Jay.

Despite that awkward first meeting, it didn't take long for the boys to warm to each other. 'It's one of those things where you try and make more jokes than you normally would – I'm sweating now at the thought of it. But we got on pretty quick, to be fair,' says Max.

A band is born

Although at first glance they didn't look like your typical boyband, actually, this was on purpose – and turned out for the best. 'When people first meet us they think we're a bit odd as we look so different,' says Jay. 'We're an unusual combination but we hope there is something for everyone.' The group was born – although it didn't have a name.

Boyband bootcamp!

With no time to waste, the boys went straight into the studio to work with Guy Chambers, who wrote 'Angels' for Robbie Williams – a very scary experience to start with! Then they headed for dance workshops with Brian Friedman, *The X Factor* choreographer. 'He's such a nice guy but he can be strict as well,' says Max. 'If you got anything wrong, he made you do press-ups and squats!'

As the training was so intensive, all the boys relocated to London and moved into a house together. Luckily for them they all got on like family almost immediately. 'If you put five randomers into a band you're either gonna hate each other or you're all going to get on. We are really, really tight,' says Tom.

The name game

Soon after moving in together, the boys were working in the studio on a track called 'Let's Get Ugly', based on the theme from the film *The Good The Bad and The Ugly*. After hearing the theme for the hundredth time, Nathan started imagining wanted posters with the faces of the group on. 'Hey!' he called to the other lads. 'How about calling ourselves "The Wanted"?' All the boys agreed it was a great idea. The Wanted were born!

On the road

With a handful of songs written and a name for themselves, the boys were ready to hit the road. Without selling any records, the boys were living off nothing and relying on fans to provide them with clothing! 'We're broke' said Siva. 'We're in rags and tags. If we want anything we have to beg and ask fans to send us clothes.'

Wearing begged threads, they supported The Saturdays for a couple of their summer dates, and launched their Schools Tour. During this time they visited schools across the country, singing up close and personal for hundreds of screaming fans! Were you one of the lucky few?

Names and faces

During this time, all the boys made very sure to remember names and faces of their first fans and tried to answer every tweet and message on Facebook. They did long days of performances and countless interviews on radio stations and TV shows.

Life in the fast lane

'The music business is 100 miles an hour,' says Max. 'It never stops and it never sleeps and it doesn't eat much either. We sleep in the car, we recline the seats and chill out and get an hour here and there. If we get four hours at home, that's a good night sleep for us. We just run on adrenaline.'

But they all knew what they wanted, and that was to be top of the charts. They wouldn't rest until they'd achieved it.

All time high

The middle of the summer drew near, and the band's first single 'All Time Low' was ready for release. They played to thousands of screaming fans at Westfield in London and were signing for fans for a mammouth six hours! But despite all the hard work, touring and preparation, they received a blow – the single wasn't getting any play on Radio 1. The boys were gutted.

'I'm devastated,' said Jay. 'I used to listen to Radio 1 all the time and it would just be the cherry on the cake for the dream, but they're just not digging us yet. Hopefully they will one day.'

Number 1!

The station didn't have much choice when just a week later 'All Time Low' went straight into the charts at Number 1! The boys were over the moon, and had a few answers for those wondering how on earth they managed to get away with it . . .

'THERE HAS BEEN A LOT OF GREAT INDIE MUSIC IN THE CHARTS IN THE PAST FEW YEARS BUT OTHER THAN JLS THERE HASN'T REALLY BEEN A GOOD BOYBAND. WE'RE A BIT OF JLS, A BIT OF TAKE THAT AND A BIT OF WESTLIFE. AND WE CAN PLAY INSTRUMENTS. IT'S EDGY POP. WE DON'T SEE JLS AS A RIVAL. TOGETHER WE CAN DO GOOD THINGS FOR BRITISH MUSIC!' TOM

Celebration time

After 'All Time Low' went to Number 1, the boys let their hair down with a five day long celebration party – all except for Nathan, who isn't old enough to drink, though he still went out and partied with them all.

After all their hard work, the boys were justified in their celebrations. The week also coincided with Tom's 22nd birthday – which gave them another excuse to party. 'We got home at 6am,' said Siva, wearing shades! Is there no end to these guys' energy?!

@ NATHAN
NATHAN LOVES NOTHING MORE THAN PLAYING THE PIANO AND SINGING.

'WE'RE JUST AVERAGE LADS, FROM WORKING-CLASS BACKGROUNDS. WE HAVEN'T CHANGED THE WAY WE LIVE. AS LONG AS WE DON'T GET CALLED "MAN BAND" JUST YET – THAT SOUNDS A BIT STRANGE!' MAX

'IT'S AN ACE THING TO BE CALLED A BOYBAND. WE WANT TO BRING BOYBANDS BACK' JAY

Heart Vacancy

After their short blowout, The Wanted went straight back to work, flying out to Croatia to film the video for their second single, 'Heart Vacancy'. 'It's about a girl who's blocking you out and you're just trying to get into her heart but she's too used to being lonely,' explained Siva. 'It's about just reaching out to her.'

YouTube hit!

Filming for the video had only just wrapped when the boys heard the news that their video for 'All Time Low' had been viewed 2.5 million times on YouTube – incredible for a group that had only been together a matter of months!

Despite the good news, there was no time to rest. The boys set about preparing tour dates and rehearsing their live show, as well as getting their debut album ready for release. 2010 was a busy year for the boys!

'WE'RE NOT YOUR TRADITIONAL BOYBAND. WE BREAK THE RULES!' TOM

BANDMATES, HOUSEMATES, FRIENDS

Since moving in together, The Wanted are around each other pretty much 24 hours a day. They sing together, eat together, play jokes on each other, and sometimes even share beds! Check out all the secrets about these five housemates!

Their first place, a five bedroom London pad, was pretty basic. The boys made sure they had the essential items in first – a football table and a darts board! 'Then a fridge full of beers and freezer full of pizzas,' laughs Tom. 'What more do you need?'

Green fingers

Although the place had a garden, the boys ended up killing the plants as they didn't water them often enough. The garden also took a turn for the smellier when Jay started throwing his pet lizard's poo out of the window! Ewww! Jay is also the member whose bedsheets smell the worst – as there's a lizard crawling over them all day . . .

Cleaner? Yes please!

The boys have a cleaner who comes in twice a week and does everything – even all the washing and ironing! But the house can be a little out of control when it comes to mess (two cleaners already quit as the house was in such a state!) But the boys are having the time of their lives. 'It's like being at college, except without the scamping for money, and making a tin of beans last all week,' says Siva. Hmmm, well boys will be boys!

★★★★★★★★★★★★★★★★★★★★★★★★★

Messiest – Max and Tom
Most likely to say something then regret it – Jay and Siva
Sweetest smelling – Max
Worst behaved – Tom

★★★★★★★★★★★★★★★★★★★★★★★★★

@ SIVA
SIVA'S FAVOURITE PLACE AT HOME IS IN FRONT OF THE FIRE. AWWW!

@ MAX
MAX HAS A PHOBIA OF DRY SPONGES – THEY MAKE HIS SKIN CRAWL!

Chillin' at home

So what do they do when they get home from playing a live set? 'Watch some TV, make some food and then I fall asleep in Max's bed!' laughs Tom. 'I won't lie to you, it's true. We wake up in the middle of the night and it's like 'Oh, I'm in Max's bed!'.

But don't worry girls, you'll never have to put up with this behaviour, as The Wanted house is a lad-pad only! 'No girls allowed!' says Max. 'Everyone hangs around in my room because I'm the only one with Sky TV.'

★★★★★★★★★★★★★★★★★★★★★★★★★

ROOM SECRETS: Siva has a TV in his room, and likes to light lots of candles to create a super-chilled atmosphere!

★★★★★★★★★★★★★★★★★★★★★★★★★

Team chef

As for who is the most annoying to live with – everyone names Tom, who always leaves the milk out of the fridge, where it turns into cheese! Eeeew! But Tom redeems himself when it comes to cooking, as he's the best of the bunch.

And who's the worst when it comes to cooking? 'Nathan!' the boys all sing together in chorus. Nathan's got a reputation for being pretty bad in the kitchen – he can't even make a Pot Noodle properly!

'TOM MAKES FOOD FOR US ALL,' SAYS MAX. 'WE'RE LIKE KIDS AND HE MAKES IT ALL.'

Jokers

Although he might be bad in the kitchen, Nathan's quite handy with a video camera, and is the self-appointed cameraman of The Wanted house. He's always sneaking into the other boys' rooms and sticking his camera in their face when they least expect it!

The other boys like playing pranks on each other too. Jay doesn't like polystyrene, so one night Siva put some under Jay's pillow. Eventually Jay fell asleep, but then leapt out of bed screaming once he discovered exactly what was rustling under his head! Jay and Tom were going to put raw bacon in Siva's shoes and let it fester and smell but they never got round to it. Urgh! There are always practical jokes going on in this house!

Home is where the heart is

Having moved to a whole new city, you'd expect the boys to be a little homesick – and you're right. They're all softies at heart and despite their big adventure, they really miss their family and friends at home. 'I really miss my parents but when you move to London it's a whole new adventure,' says Tom. 'When we do get time off, we do go home and spend time with our friends and family. We had Sunday off to celebrate our chart position!'

GIRLS, DATING, LOVE

Fans

If there's one thing The Wanted have done that sets them apart from the other boybands out there, it's that they're totally in love with their fans! Each boy spends hours and hours every day on Twitter, answering tweets from fans. They dedicate their Wanted Wednesday webcast every week to answer questions that fans send in. These boys know how important it is to keep up that bond – so they're online nearly 24/7!

Before the boys had their number one, they could stop in the street and chat to fans. But since they hit the top of the charts, things have been a lot more difficult – those boys really have become wanted!

★

'WE'VE HAD TO GET MORE SECURITY GUARDS NOW, BECAUSE WHEREVER THERE ARE FANS WE STOP AND SPEAK TO THEM, BUT THE LAST FEW DAYS WE HAVEN'T ALWAYS HAD TIME OR IT'S NOT ALWAYS BEEN SAFE FOR US TO DO SO.' TOM

Respect the fans

After they reached number one in the chart, the first thing the boys did was to stand outside the Radio 1 studios and chat to their fans, who were waiting outside to support the group. 'We make a lot of effort because we all genuinely like talking to our fans,' says Jay.

Going from being relative unknowns to household names in a matter of weeks has been a surreal experience for the boys, who have seen their Facebook fans and Twitter follower numbers go through the roof!

'It's a bit weird because we don't see ourselves as famous - we're just five lads that are enjoying ourselves,' says Tom. 'It's odd when the paps are chasing us on motorbikes, or when girls cry when they meet us - it's like 'we're ok, we don't bite!"

Stage invasion

All the boys are very attached to their fans and humbled by the amount of support the public have given them, especially all those screaming girls! And one of the school gigs that the boys did ended up with the pupils storming the stage – very rock 'n' roll!

Famous friends

It's not only the public who've gone Wanted crazy – the boys have found fans in famous folk too! Alexandra Burke, Pixie Lott (who was seen out drinking with the lads), Joe McElderry, Tinie Tempah, Chipmunk and JLS have all publicly supported the group. That's quite a fanbase to be starting off with! They also know The Saturdays quite well, having supported the girls at a number of gigs and also sharing the same management.

@ JAY
IF JAY COULD MEET ANY CELEBRITY, IT WOULD'VE BEEN MICHAEL JACKSON.

@ TOM
IF TOM COULD SPEND A DAY
WITH ANYONE, DEAD OR ALIVE,
HE'D PICK JOHN LENNON FROM
THE BEATLES.

Romance rumours

Unsurprisingly, the boys have also already been the centre of a number of romance rumours - these guys can't go anywhere wthout causing a stir! When the lads first met Leona Lewis during a night out celebrating the success of 'All Time Low' at a club in London, they immediately hit it off so the press had a field day! There has also been speculation in the tabloids about Max and Vanessa from The Saturdays, but the boys haven't confirmed any of the rumours, so there's hope for us yet!

★★★★★★★★★★★★★★★

Q. Would you date a fan?
A. THE WANTED: 'Definitely!'

★★★★★★★★★★★★★★★

@ TOM

TOM'S DAD IS SO POPULAR AMONGST WANTED FANS, HE EVEN HAS HIS OWN FACEBOOK FANPAGE!

And even Siva, who has a long term girlfriend, has been attracting the A-listers. Siva and the rest of the band were hanging out with none other than Princess Rih Rih! Rihanna performed at Capital FM's Summertime Ball as did The Wanted, and apparently they partied together after the show. Since then rumours of chemistry flew around the tabloid press, but there's no romance there as Siva is loved up with his girlfriend.

The rest of the boys, however, are blissfully single! 'We're pretty busy,' explains Max. 'If we go for a drink when we finish a gig, there are nice ladies around, and we might socialise, but usually once we've finished a gig we're in the back of a van travelling somewhere else.'

Whenever the boys are seen out partying, they always turn on the charm for the girls that are around – except Siva, who's polite, but is devoted to his girlfriend. What a sweetie!

★★★★★★★★★★★★★★★★★
No matter how much female attention Nathan gets now, he's unlikely to top his first kiss! When he was eight years old he won a competition to appear with Britney on a TV show. He asked her for a kiss, and she landed him one on the cheek! 'I was a hero for years at school,' says NATHAN!
★★★★★★★★★★★★★★★★★

@ NATHAN
NATHAN CAN PLAY PIANO AND THE BAGPIPES!

@ MAX
IF MAX LOOKS FAMILIAR, IT'S PROBABLY FROM WHEN HIS BAND AVENUE PERFORMED ON *THE X FACTOR* – BUT WERE BOOTED OUT FOR HAVING A MANAGER.

@ JAY
JAY HAS A PET LIZARD – A TREAT THAT HE BOUGHT AFTER THE GROUP WENT TO NUMBER 1!

@ SIVA
SIVA IS ONE OF EIGHT SIBLINGS IN AN ALL-SINGING, ALL-DANCING, MEGA TALENTED FAMILY! HIS TWIN BROTHER AND HIS ELDEST BROTHER ALSO AUDITIONED FOR THE WANTED.

THE MUSIC

It's amazing that five lads who are all so gorgeous are super-talented too. Some guys get all the luck!

Although Siva is nicknamed Bambi because he's not the best dancer, he's been playing guitar, singing and writing songs for years and his talent shines through. In his audition he sang 'Home' by Michael Buble along with a song he had written himself. He also had to dance for the judges, so his singing must have been pretty impressive!

Multi-talented boys!

All the other boys also passed the auditions with flying colours – either for their ability with musical instruments (like Nathan and Tom), their dancing prowess (like Jay), or their smouldering onstage charisma (like Max). One thing all the boys share in common, they have voices like angels!

The boys have drawn comparisons to one of the UK's original boybands, Take That. 'I love the fact that Take That have come back,' says Tom. 'I was so surprised when 'Patience' came out. I've got massive respect for Gary Barlow in particular. To reinvent a new sound for them was incredible.'

★★★★★★★★★★★★★★★★★★★★★★★★★

Q. If we were going to compare The Wanted to Take That, who would be who – in terms of personality?
A. JAY: 'People say I'm like Howard as I'm the dancer, and indie kid Siva is Jason, the model with good looks. Max is Robbie, a bit of a lad. Nathan is Gary, with all the piano playing; he's a songwriter. And Tom would have to be cheeky Mark!'

★★★★★★★★★★★★★★★★★★★★★★★★★

Although joining a boyband may have seemed like a strange choice, every member of The Wanted firmly believe that boybands are back – and they're cool again, thanks to rivals JLS!

In the studio

The boys were lucky enough to have famous producers writing songs for the album – amongst them Guy Chambers, Taio Cruz, Wayne Hector, Steve Mac and even Cathy Dennis! But given how musically talented the boys already are, they worked on a lot of the material themselves – every member of the group apart from Jay had written songs before joining the band so it was all very natural to them.

They started working on the album in early 2010, and recorded 40 songs in total. They never expected to be working alongside such big name producers. All the boys have very different tastes in music: Tom likes Oasis and the Stereophonics; Max is a big Elvis fan; Jay likes folk like Cat Stevens and indie; Siva likes Motown; and Nathan likes R'n'B like John Legend and Boyz II Men. Quite a mixture! Combining all these boys together has led to a great mixed album that will keep everyone happy.

Something for everyone

'There's something for everyone on the new album,' says Tom. 'There's mid-tempo tracks, there's beat tracks, then you've got your power ballads as well. We've been lucky to work with such amazing writers.'

So what about the singles? "All Time Low' is generally about when you can't get a girl out of your head,' says Max. All the boys loved it the first time they heard it. 'We heard a lot of songs and tried writing a lot of songs, but that one just summed us up – that was the song we wanted to introduce us to the world!' says Jay.

And as for 'Heart Vacancy' – 'It's slower, with a big beat . . . a ballad,' Max goes on. 'It's one for the girls, but hopefully lads will like the beat in it. It was written by Wayne Hector. He wrote 'Beat Again' for JLS.'

'WE WERE JUST AFTER A TOP 40 HIT — WE WOULD HAVE CELEBRATED IN A MASSIVE WAY IF WE'D JUST REACHED THE TOP 40, SO YOU CAN IMAGINE WHAT THE CELEBRATION WAS LIKE WHEN WE GOT TO NUMBER 1!' NATHAN

Releasing the album

Even though releasing the album towards the end of 2010 (and putting it up against Joe McElderry and Take That) was a gamble, The Wanted's management knew the album was going to smash it in the charts! Especially being released in special edition with five different covers – one for every member of the band! But the boys were never worried about the album's release as they had already achieved way more than they ever expected to.

'We just have to do our own thing,' said Max. *The X Factor*'s huge and Take That are leagues ahead of us. We just do what we do and worry about ourselves rather than anyone else. We'll just stick to our guns.'

Let's hope those boys keep doing that – it's certainly worked for them so far!

The Wanted versus JLS...

Although everyone's been calling The Wanted 'the new JLS', for the boys, there's just no comparison.

'It's hugely flattering – they've absolutely smashed it,' says Jay. 'If anything they are inspirations, because they've done it in a big way and brought the whole boyband thing back, if they hadn't done that I don't know if we could have done it. I think we'll just jump on their band wagon!'

Tom agrees: 'We're quite different bands really, and I think their fans accept and appreciate that we aren't trying to be them, we're just trying to do our own thing and be ourselves and hopefully people will appreciate and like that.'

All of the band have nothing but admiration for JLS. 'To be even mentioned in the same breath as JLS is a compliment,' says Siva. 'And I guess it didn't take them long to get to the top!'

★★★★★★★★★★★★★★★

Q. How do you write songs?
A. NATHAN: 'I just write about my feelings on the day, so sometimes it'd be a ballad or sometimes just a bit rocky - just let your feelings pour out onto paper. Or write about friends' situations or someone you love. It's always best to get a catchy little hook that people will remember.'

★★★★★★★★★★★★★★★

THE FUTURE

Hit singles, a debut album, gigs galore and moving into their second house together – it's already been such a busy year for The Wanted! But they've got so many plans, and even more things to look forward to.

The future's bright

Well, it's definitely been a rollercoaster ride that's brought The Wanted lads to where they are today! Picked from different corners of the country and touring hundreds of schools trying to make a name for themselves to sell-out concerts in front of thousands of screaming fans, these five lads have come such a long way. 2010 has seen them release number one bestselling singles, as well as an incredible debut album packed with hits and performing at sold-out gigs across the UK and Europe as well as at all the coolest events and festivals – we can't wait to see what they've got lined up for 2011!

Both feet on the ground

But rather than letting all the fame go to their heads, Nathan, Max, Siva, Jay and Tom remain the down to earth guys they've always been. None of the boys come from starry families – all the boys were chosen for their individual talents – so they all know what life is like when the cameras aren't capturing your every move which helps them keep both feet on the ground.

Next stop, America!

But that doesn't mean there is a shortage of ambition. The boys want to conquer America, and perform with some of the world's biggest artists, including Eminem, Pixie Lott and Lady Gaga! 'Gaga – she's amazing,' gushes Jay. 'She makes actual masterpieces. I'd be really interested to she what she's like in real life.' And how about a collaboration with The Saturdays? Gorgeous boyband + gorgeous girlband = perfect superband! Here's hoping that is on the cards!

WHAT DO THE STARS HOLD FOR THE WANTED?

TOM was born on 4 August and JAY was born on 24 July so they're both LEOs. Leos are ruled by their hearts, are charismatic and positive-thinking. They survive life's stormy times with style and good humour – so whatever 2011 throws at The Wanted, Tom and Jay will be good guys to have around!

NATHAN was born on 18 April so he's an ARIES. Those born under Aries are often adventurous, confident and outgoing. But they can be innocent and naïve too – awwww! Being the youngest in the band, Nathan will at least have the others to look out for him!

MAX was born on 6 September so he's a VIRGO. Virgos are known for being compassionate, caring and often creative . . . all this behind the tough boy exterior! Could he be the perfect guy?!

SIVA was born on 16 November so he's a SCORPIO. Those born under Scorpio often have intense and dramatic relationships, and are thought to be wise – sounds like Siva.

Centre stage

The boys love to perform for their fans and following their huge success across the country, there are rumours of a full UK tour soon as well. Watch out for announcements from the band and you could get yourself tickets to see the boys live in action on stage – yay!

The only way is up!

What about those rumours about the group splitting and all going solo? Well, Nathan has plans to go back to college and finish his A Levels and Max would like to get into acting someday. But not yet. One thing's for sure: For the time being, the boys are staying true to their word and staying together! Phew!

So for the foreseeable future, this cheeky fivesome are going to be concentrating on doing what we love them best for – giving us killer pop tunes and killer smiles. Keep it up boys!

PICTURE CREDITS
All pictures courtesy of Getty Images

ACKNOWLEDGEMENTS
Posy Edwards would like to thank Helia Phoenix, Jane Sturrock,
Helen Ewing, Clare Hennessy, Nicola Crossley, Hannah Lewis,
Rich Carr, and Smith & Gilmour

First published in hardback in Great Britain in 2010 by Orion Books
an imprint of the Orion Publishing Group Ltd Orion House,
5 Upper St Martin's Lane, London WC2H 9EA
An Hachette UK Company

10 9 8 7 6 5 4 3 2 1

A CIP catalogue record for this book is available from the British Library.

ISBN: 978 1 4091 3264 6

Designed by Smith & Gilmour
Printed in Spain by Cafosa

The Orion Publishing Group's policy is to use papers that are natural, renewable
and recyclable and made from wood grown in sustainable forests. The logging and
manufacturing processes are expected to conform to the environmental regulations
of the country of origin.

Every effort has been made to fulfil requirements with regard to reproducing
copyright material. The author and publisher will be glad to rectify any omissions
at the earliest opportunity.

www.orionbooks.co.uk